"SHHH"
IS A FOUR LETTER WORD

"LAUGHS FOR LIBRARY LOVERS"

By Andy Gibbons
& Jeanne Nelson

PUBLISHED BY
  R&E PUBLISHERS
  P.O. BOX 2008
  SARATOGA, CA 95070

LIBRARY OF CONGRESS
  CATALOG CARD NO.
      83-62296
  I.S.B.N. 0-88247-702-1

TO ORDER SEND
     9.95 + 1.50
  SHIPPING TO
     R&E
  P.O. BOX 2008
  SARATOGA, CA
     95070

LIBRARIES ARE OFTEN
PICTURED AS SOMBER, MUSTY
PLACES WHERE MYSTERIOUS
MATERIALS ARE ESOTERICALLY
FILED BY CULTISTS VERSED
IN THE BLACK ARTS OF
DEWEY AND L.C.

IT MAY BE TRUE. WHAT
IS ALSO TRUE IS THAT
LIBRARIES ARE FUN PLACES
WHERE HUMOROUS, EVEN ROLLICKING THINGS HAPPEN,
AND WHERE ONLY "SHHH!" STILLS HERETICAL LAUGHTER.

LET IMA OVERDEW, STAUNCH LIBRARIAN; TARA
LITTLEPAGE, MODERN MEDIA SPECIALIST; AND MARK
PLACES, COMPUTERIZED INFORMATION TECHNOLOGIST,
SHOW YOU SUCH A LAUGHING
LIBRARY.

SELF DECLARED AUTHORITIES
ON THIS LAUGHTER ARE THE
CREATORS, ANDY GIBBONS AND
JEANNIE NELSON. ANDY
TEACHES AT A UNIVERSITY,
AND JEANNIE "LIBRARYS" IN
A HIGH SCHOOL MEDIA CENTER.

BOTH OF THEM ENJOY HUMOR RAMPANT AND
PUN IRREVERENT. WHEN THEY COULD NO LONGER
CONTAIN THEMSELVES, THIS BOOK BURST FORTH....

SO, NEXT TIME YOU VISIT YOUR FAVORITE
LIBRARY, REMEMBER THAT "SHHH IS A FOUR-
LETTER WORD."

WHEN I STARTED, WE DIDN'T GET COFFEE BREAKS!

OF COURSE WE HAVE SOMETHING ON WIND
ENERGY - LOOK UNDER "ATMOSPHERE- USEFUL
ASPECTS."

YOUR BROTHER IN THE MARINES CHECKED THOSE OUT WHEN HE WAS YOUR AGE – AND YOU'RE RETURNING THEM NOW?

Y'KNOW, I DIDN'T DRINK BEFORE
I BECAME A LIBRARIAN!

J.NELSON '82

THERE'S THE CARD CATALOG, RIGHT
THERE!

ALL I SAID WAS, "WHAT A LUCIOUS PEAR!"

WHAT'S MY DAD MEAN - I WAS "CONCEIVED IN THE STACKS ?"

I KNOW ABOUT THE BIRDS AND BEES — I WANT TO KNOW ABOUT HUMAN REPRODUCTION!

"THE APATHY YOU'VE SHOWN LATELY BOTHERS ME!" "WHO CARES!"

$2,238.26 DOES SEEM A LITTLE HIGH FOR A BOOK FINE - HOW LONG DID YOU SAY YOU'VE HAD THE BOOK?

WE HAVE SOME LOVELY BOOKS TO
DONATE TO THE LIBRARY.

BUT MOM - WHAT DO YOU MEAN, I DON'T
LOOK LIKE A LIBRARIAN?

J. NELSON '82

YOU MEET THE MOST INTERESTING PATRONS
IN THE HUMAN SEXUALITY SECTION!

NO MORE T-SHIRTS
IN THIS LIBRARY!

WILL THIS BE ALL?

EXCUSE ME - WHATS THE DATE TODAY?

YOU NEED A PHOTOCOPIER REPAIRED?

THERES TARZAN AND JANE!

MEN   OTHER   WOME

...STROOMS →

J. NELSON '82

DO YOU HAVE SOMETHING ON ACROPHOBIA?

I NEED INFORMATION, MAC,! STUFF ON
INFERIORITY COMPLEXES.

BOY - ITS AS QUIET AS A LIBRARY HERE!

THIS BOOK IS A COMMUNIST PLOT!

THIS TIME IT WASN'T PROGRESS - OUR FUNDING WAS OUT.

GUESS WHO REALLY CLEANS UP AROUND
HERE!

IS THIS WHATS KNOWN AS A BINDING
AGREEMENT?

ALL I EVER GET FOR CHRISTMAS IS
BOOKS, BOOKS, BOOKS.

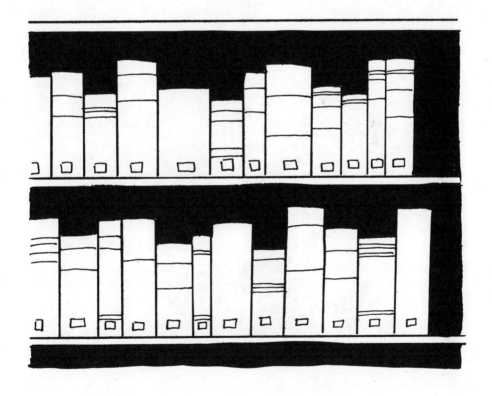

MEDICAL BOOKS
PLEASE LIMIT
YOURSELF
5 SYMPTOMS ONLY

J. NELSON '82

DR. SMITHS BOOKS ARE N<u>EV</u>ER TO BE
DUE ON WEDNESDAY!

HERE'S THAT "DIFFERENT DRUMMER" I
MARCH TO!

DONT YOU THINK ITS TIME
WE WENT HOME?

AND TO THINK, I USED TO LIKE BOOKS

WEED?! NEVER!!

IMA'S REALLY EDGY LATELY!

READ? WHO HAS TIME TO READ!

BETTER HIDE THAT PROJECTOR — OR THEY'LL
CALL US A MEDIA CENTER!

I CAN'T SOLVE YOUR PROBLEM —
I <u>AM</u> YOUR PROBLEM!

EVERYONE SHOULD LEARN A FOREIGN
LANGUAGE

IM OVERDUE AT THAT BIG LIBRARY
IN THE SKY!

ITS A MADHOUSE — HOW ARE THINGS
IN YOUR LIBRARY?

DUCK? NO- LOOK UNDER WATER OWL.

WHATS <u>WRONG</u> WITH THIS T-SHIRT?

IT'S EASY - IF I LIKE THEM, THEY'RE MATURE.

HER BOOKS AREN'T THE ONLY THING THATS OVERDUE!

BUT ALL HE DOES IS SIT AND READ AND SMILE.

WHEN SOMEONE ASKS FOR DANTE, WE DO NOT TELL THEM TO "GO TO HELL!"

HMM... NOTHING ON TORTOISES, BUT <u>LOTS</u> ON TURTLES!

WE'VE GOT TO GET ALL THOSE OVERDUE
BOOKS IN — THERE ARE TOO MANY BOOKS OUT.

WE'VE GOT TO INCREASE CIRCULATION—
MORE BOOKS TO MORE PEOPLE!

"NEPOTISM"? LOOK UNDER "RELATIVITY"!

PUT THOSE RODS BACK!

J.NELSON '82

SO THIS IS A SILENCER! MY, MY, MY!

SOMEHOW I DON'T THINK ITS EQUALIZATION MONIES!

SOMETIMES I WISH THERE WERE NO WORLD RECORD BOOKS!

THERE IS NO DIALOUGE ON THIS FILM!

ITS HARD TO BELIEVE ITS OCTOBER
ALREADY !

WHEN ARE THE BANKING BOOKS?
IN THE HIGH INTEREST SECTION.

MR. PLACES - THESE MICROFICHE ARE
<u>NEATO</u>!

"DO YOU HAVE ANYTHING ON ATHEISM?"
"GOD, NO!"

HE'S HERE RELIGIOUSLY EVERYDAY!

WOW - SUPERGLUE SURE LOOKS WEIRD
UP CLOSE.

ITS- THE NEWEST "HOW-TO" BOOK-
HOW TO NOT APPEAR TO BE DOING WRONG.

DO YOU HAVE ANYTHING ON SWINGING?
TRY THE 700's!

TRY THE 200'S IF THAT DOESN'T WORK.

I JUST KNOW THEY'RE NOT KEEPING THE
SHELVES IN ORDER!

CONGRADULATIONS! YOU'RE MY 1,000TH
FOOLISH QUESTION!

J.NELSON'82

ITS HARDER TO FIND A COMMITED
LIBRARIAN THAN ONE THAT SHOULD BE
COMMITED.

OH, RELAX - ITS ONLY MY COSTUME FOR
THE HALLOWEEN PARTY!

IM A MEDIA SPECIALIST, SHE'S A
LIBRARIAN, AND HES AN INFORMATION
TECHNICIAN.

BUT YOU SAID WE COULD BRING OUR
LUNCH.

J. NELSON '82

SOMEHOW IT ALWAYS SEEMS _INFANCY_
SHOULD COME BEFORE _ADULTERY_.

SAYING "SHHH" IS A DIRTY THANKLESS
JOB, BUT SOMEBODY HAS TO DO IT!

THE RACE IS NOT ALWAYS TO THE
SWIFT—BOOK, PLEASE!

WHY IS <u>EVERYTHING</u> DUE ON THE SAME DAY?

ONE THING FOR SURE - YOUR <u>CIRCULATION</u> IS EXCELLENT.

YOU'LL LIKE THIS WALLPAPER —
IT LOOKS LIKE SHELVES OF BOOKS.

AND WHATS <u>WRONG</u> WITH LAVENDER
SPINE LABELS?

WE'VE HAD BAD LUCK WITH OUR LIBRARIANS—
ONE QUIT AND THE OTHER DIDN'T.

I HAVE TO RETURN THESE RODS TO THE CARD
CATALOG IN THE MORNING.

SHE'S THE LAMB, I'M THE CRAB, ANDS HE'S
THE TURKEY.

J. NELSON '82

WE DO <u>NOT</u> FILE BIORHYTHM UNDER BIRTHCONTROL

NEVER SCHEDULE LIBRARY BOARD MEETINGS
WEDNESDAYS! THERE ARE 3 DOCTORS
ON THE BOARD.

ALL RIGHT — WHO DID THIS?

I'M RIGHT HERE IF YOU NEED ME!

THISH BOOK ON HOME BREWING ISH
WUNNERFUL!

WHERE'S THAT NEATO BOOK ON STRINGING
TENNIS RACKETS?

ITS THE TIRE UNDER THE OVERSIZE
BOOKS NATURALLY.

YOU SHOULD SEE THE NEW GRAFFITI !

I THINK WE ARE "ENTITLED" TO CUT OFF
DONATIONS FOR AWHILE!

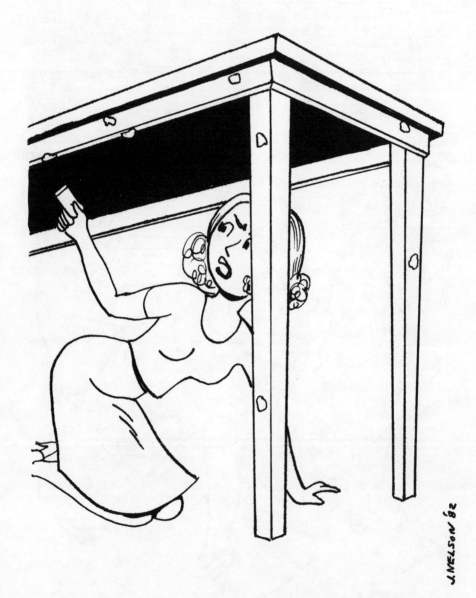

JUST WHAT IS IT WE <u>DON'T</u> DO
AROUND HERE?

YOU CAN SURE TELL IMA USED TO BE
A HOME EC TEACHER.

MY HERO

WHAT A <u>GORGEOUS</u> PAIR OF SHOES!

NO THIS IS NOT WHERE YOU GET YOUR
BLOOD PRESSURE CHECKED.

J. NELSON 82

ITS JUST SOMETHING I ALWAYS WANTED
TO DO!

WE GOT OUR GRANT!

IT SAYS "WATCH FOR THE NEXT VOLUME
OF LIBRARY CARTOONS."

J. NELSON '82